LEWIS HINE

the
empire
state
building
photographs

■

■ a book of 30 postcards

Pomegranate Artbooks
Box 6099
Rohnert Park, CA 94927

Pomegranate Europe Ltd.
Fullbridge House, Fullbridge
Maldon, Essex CM9 4LE
England

ISBN 1-56640-024-4
Pomegranate Catalog No. A610

Pomegranate publishes books of
postcards on a wide range of subjects.
Please write to the publisher for more information.

Designed by Harrah Argentine
Printed in Korea
06 05 04 03 02 01 00   13 12 11 10 9 8 7 6

To facilitate detachment of the postcards from this book, fold each card along its perforation line before tearing.

LEWIS HINE

Lewis Hine's (1874–1940) early photographic career was largely dedicated to documenting the exploitation of the workplace and the social evils of the industrial revolution. From 1904 until the end of World War I, he worked as a "social photographer," creating powerful and widely reproduced images of immigrants at Ellis Island, iron and steel workers in Pittsburgh and, as staff photographer for the National Child Labor Committee, the lives of working children all over the country.

After the war Hine turned to "positive documentation" in an effort to show the human side of industrialization. As a part of that effort he created a series of critically acclaimed individual "Work Portraits," which led to a 1930 commission to photograph the construction of the Empire State Building. Hine documented the project from the ground up, going to great and dizzying lengths including being swung out in a cement bucket to get good shots of the work in progress. When the project was completed, Hine combined a number of the images with some of the Work Portraits in *Men at Work*, a pioneering photographic picture book. Today Hine's amazing photographs of the Empire State Building constitute a priceless record of a memorable event in American history. This book of postcards presents thirty of Hine's photographs from this project. ■

LEWIS HINE
the empire state building photographs

■ A derrick man

Pomegranate Box 808022 Petaluma CA 94975

LEWIS HINE
the empire state building photographs

■ A hoisting gang at work on 34th Street elevation

Pomegranate Box 808022 Petaluma CA 94975

LEWIS HINE
the empire state building photographs

■ A burner cutting a beam with his acetylene torch

Pomegranate Box 808022 Petaluma CA 94975

LEWIS HINE
the empire state building photographs

■ Putting a beam in place

Pomegranate   Box 808022   Petaluma   CA 94975

LEWIS HINE
the empire state building photographs

■ An inspector on the job

Pomegranate Box 808022 Petaluma CA 94975

LEWIS HINE
the empire state building photographs

- "Topping out" the Empire State Building

Pomegranate Box 808022 Petaluma CA 94975

LEWIS HINE
the empire state building photographs

■ A view of the Manhattan skyline and the Hudson River
from the George Washington Bridge

Pomegranate   Box 808022   Petaluma   CA 94975

LEWIS HINE
the empire state building photographs

■ A derrick man

Pomegranate   Box 808022   Petaluma   CA 94975

LEWIS HINE
the empire state building photographs

- A view of the Empire State Building from inside the tower of the Chrysler Building

Pomegranate Box 808022 Petaluma CA 94975

LEWIS HINE
the empire state building photographs

■ A view of downtown Manhattan from the Empire
State Building

Pomegranate   Box 808022   Petaluma   CA 94975

LEWIS HINE
the empire state building photographs

- A view of the Empire State Building from 34th
  Street and Madison Avenue

Pomegranate Box 808022 Petaluma CA 94975

LEWIS HINE
the empire state building photographs

■ Riveters at work

Pomegranate   Box 808022   Petaluma   CA 94975

LEWIS HINE
the empire state building photographs

■ Mason at work

Pomegranate Box 808022 Petaluma CA 94975

LEWIS HINE
the empire state building photographs

- A member of the derrick crew

Pomegranate   Box 808022   Petaluma   CA 94975

LEWIS HINE
the empire state building photographs

■ A break from work

Pomegranate Box 808022 Petaluma CA 94975

LEWIS HINE
the empire state building photographs

■ A break from work

Pomegranate Box 808022 Petaluma CA 94975

LEWIS HINE
the empire state building photographs

■ Constructing the frame of the observatory tower

Pomegranate Box 808022 Petaluma CA 94975

LEWIS HINE
the empire state building photographs

■ Derrick crew hoisting a beam

Pomegranate Box 808022 Petaluma CA 94975

LEWIS HINE
the empire state building photographs

- A view of midtown Manhattan from the Empire State Building

Pomegranate Box 808022 Petaluma CA 94975

LEWIS HINE
the empire state building photographs

■ Machinist at work

Pomegranate Box 808022 Petaluma CA 94975

LEWIS HINE
the empire state building photographs

■ Putting a beam in place

Pomegranate Box 808022 Petaluma CA 94975

LEWIS HINE
the empire state building photographs

■ On the frame of the observatory tower

Pomegranate   Box 808022   Petaluma   CA 94975

LEWIS HINE
the empire state building photographs

■ Machinist at work

Pomegranate Box 808022 Petaluma CA 94975

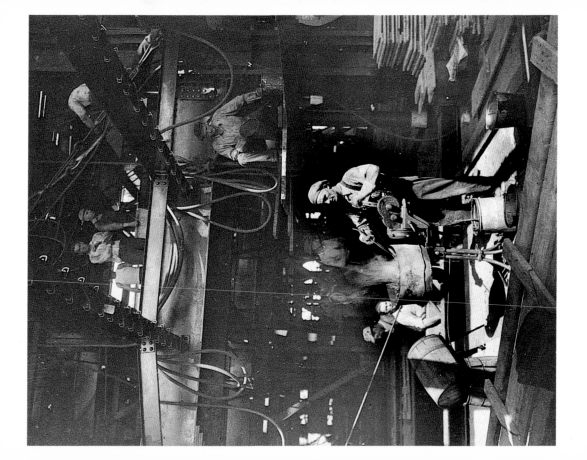

LEWIS HINE
the empire state building photographs

■ A heater getting bolts red-hot to toss to riveters

Pomegranate Box 808022 Petaluma CA 94975

LEWIS HINE
the empire state building photographs

■ Putting a beam in place

Pomegranate Box 808022 Petaluma CA 94975

LEWIS HINE
the empire state building photographs

■ A bolter at work

Pomegranate   Box 808022   Petaluma   CA 94975

LEWIS HINE
the empire state building photographs

■ At work on the structure

Pomegranate   Box 808022   Petaluma   CA 94975

LEWIS HINE
the empire state building photographs

■ A pause in work

Pomegranate   Box 808022   Petaluma   CA 94975

LEWIS HINE
the empire state building photographs

■ Bolters waiting for a new beam

Pomegranate Box 808022 Petaluma CA 94975

LEWIS HINE
the empire state building photographs

- The Sky Boy

Pomegranate Box 808022 Petaluma CA 94975